KNOWLEDGE ENCYCLOPEDIA
SOLAR SYSTEM
SPACE

© Wonder House Books 2025

All rights reserved. No part of this book may be reproduced or transmitted in any form by any means, electronic or mechanical, including photocopying and recording, or by any information storage and retrieval system except as may be expressly permitted in writing by the publisher.

(An imprint of Prakash Books)

contact@wonderhousebooks.com

Disclaimer: The information contained in this encyclopedia has been collated with inputs from subject experts. All information contained herein is true to the best of the Publisher's knowledge.

ISBN : 9789390391424

Table of Contents

The Amazing Solar System	3
Our Celestial Neighbourhood	4–5
The Great Debate: Geocentric Or Heliocentric?	6
The Majestic Milky Way	7
The Scintillating Sun	8–9
Mercury: The Smallest and the Fastest Planet	10
Venus: The Hot Planet	11
Earth: The Habitable Planet	12–13
Earth's Imaginary Lines	14–15
Earth's Movements	16–17
Earth's Moon	18–19
Phases of the Moon	20
Exploring Mars: The Red Planet	21
Jupiter: A Giant Among Planets	22–23
Saturn: The Ringed Giant	24
Uranus: The Planet that Spins Sideways	25
Neptune: The Windy Planet	26–27
The Kuiper Belt and the Oort Cloud	28–29
The Dwarf Planets	30–31
Word Check	32

THE AMAZING SOLAR SYSTEM

Our solar system consists of the Sun—a star, and all the bodies orbiting around it. These objects mainly comprise the planets, which are the largest bodies in the solar system besides the Sun. Then there are moons, asteroids, meteoroids, comets, and other celestial objects.

The solar system exists within the spiral Milky Way galaxy, which is made up of several hundred billion stars. Although the Sun is extremely important to us and without it, life would be unlikely on our planet, in the larger scheme of the galaxy and the universe, it is just an average-sized star, one of the billion stars in the Milky Way.

The eight planets of the solar system are Mercury, Venus, Earth, Mars, Jupiter, Saturn, Uranus, and Neptune—in order of their distance from the Sun. The first four inner planets are rocky or terrestrial planets. From the four outer region planets, Jupiter and Saturn are gas giants, whereas Uranus and Neptune are ice giants. Pluto, once considered a planet, has recently been given the status of a dwarf planet.

The asteroid belt (lying between Mars and Jupiter), the Kuiper Belt, and the Oort Cloud beyond the orbit of Neptune are the three other regions considered a part of the solar system.

Scientists fascinated by this wondrous and largely unexplored solar system are always looking for ways to reach out to the stars and other bodies in the Milky Way and beyond, so that they get answers to their numerous questions!

▲ *All planets, except Earth, are named after gods from Roman and Greek mythologies*

Our Celestial Neighbourhood

Have you ever gazed into the sky and wondered what magic and mystery lies beyond Earth's atmosphere in our cosmic neighbourhood? We know that the Sun, the big ball of fire we see during the day, is the heart of our solar system. But how was the solar system created and how did it grow? What is it made up of? What makes our solar system such an amazing, awe-inspiring arena?

▲ *An artist's recreation of our majestic solar system*

⭐ Formation of the Solar System

Nearly 4.6 billion years ago, there existed a thin cloud of **stellar dust**, which was part of a larger cloud or **nebula**. One day, the cloud collapsed, possibly due to the after-effects of an exploding star which made it crumble. It fell in upon itself and created a spherical disc of matter which surrounded it. Near its centre, gravity began to pull material inwards so that the immense pressure at the core of the spherical disc that was caused by this material forced hydrogen atoms to merge into helium, which in turn produced a large amount of energy—and voila! The Sun was born. The Sun pulled more than 99 per cent of the matter in the disc towards the centre, but some remained.

Next came planet formation that was rapid. Some of the leftover matter fused together due to gravity. Big objects banged against one another, forming larger objects, until they became huge enough to form spheres or planets, including **dwarf planets**. Earth and other rocky planets remained close to the Sun, as those with ice and gaseous materials could not exist near such heat. The gas and other giant ice planets, therefore, formed farther away from the Sun. This is how the solar system was formed.

👤 In Real Life

It is very likely that there are tens of billions of other solar systems in the Milky Way. So far, scientists have found more than 2,900 **planetary systems** (stars with confirmed planets) in the Milky Way galaxy.

▶ *An artist's rendering of a planetary system. The bright spot at the centre is the Sun*

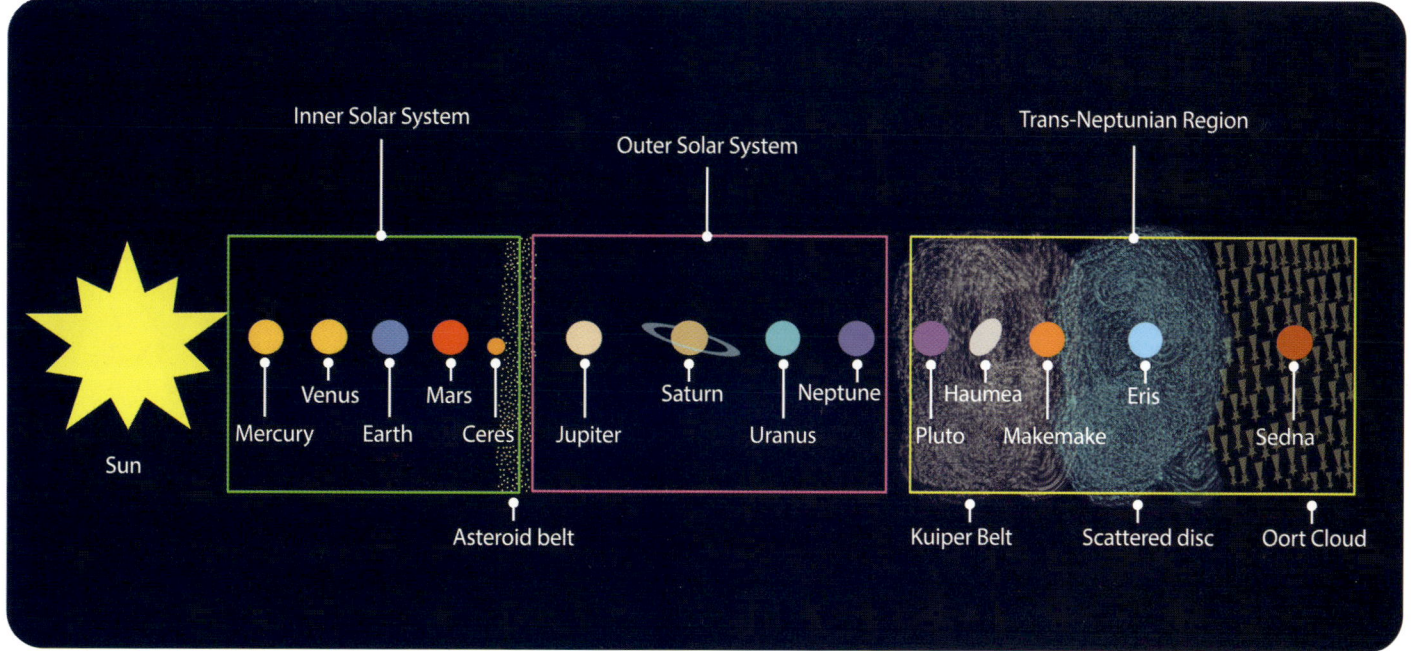

▲ The illustration shows the various celestial objects comprising our solar system in the different zones

⭐ Composition of the Solar System

The Sun is the central object within the solar system. It influences the movement of all other bodies due to its gravitational force. Besides the eight major planets that orbit around the Sun, the solar system comprises approximately 170 known moons (or planetary satellites), innumerable asteroids, comets and icy bodies. Asteroids are small, rocky objects leftover from the formation of the solar system. They are sometimes referred to as minor planets or planetoids. Asteroids orbit the Sun and are mainly found in the asteroid belt region between Mars and Jupiter. Most of them are about 1,000 kilometres or less in diameter. Asteroids and comets help us figure out the story of our very busy solar system. Astronomers believe that Jupiter's gravity prevented these pieces from clumping together into a planet. The vastness of the solar system also consists of **interplanetary medium**, thinly scattered matter that exists between the planets and other bodies as well as the forces (e.g., magnetic and electric) that are present in this region of space.

🏅 Incredible Individuals

Hipparchus was a Greek astronomer who helped develop astronomy as a mathematical science. His most significant contribution is his work on the orbits of the Sun and the Moon as well as the measurement of their sizes and distances from Earth. Hipparchus also studied eclipses. He tried to clarify how the Sun is able to travel with a steady speed along a consistent circular path and yet able to cause seasons which are unequal in duration.

▶ Hipparchus (or Hipparchos) was one of the greatest astronomers of the ancient world and contributed significantly to this field, making several noteworthy astronomical observations

The Great Debate
Geocentric or Heliocentric?

Ideas about the solar system have been different and have changed several times throughout history. Before the invention of the telescope, astronomers had to depend on gathering information from celestial objects that could be seen with the naked eye. This obviously limited their knowledge about the solar system. For several centuries, Earth was considered the center of the solar system. It was only much later that scientists realised this was not true and accepted the Sun as the center of the solar system.

▲ An early astronomical telescope. The first person to turn the telescope skyward was the famous astronomer Galileo

The Geocentric Model

It is a theory regarding the structure of the solar system where Earth is considered to be at the centre of it all. Ancient Greek and Egyptian astronomers, Aristotle and Ptolemy (2nd century CE) are chiefly responsible for promoting the geocentric model which prevailed for more than 1,000 years!

According to this system, Earth is stationary and is the centre of the universe while the Sun, planets, and stars revolve around Earth.

◀ This ancient chart shows the solar system with Earth at the centre as per Ptolemy's geocentric model of the solar system

The Heliocentric Model

This system is a cosmological model where the Sun is considered to be at the center of the solar system or the universe. As per this model, Earth and the other bodies revolve around the Sun. Back in the 5th century BCE, a few Greek philosophers had guessed this, but this belief was not recognised until much later, when Nicolaus Copernicus (1473–1543) changed the model of the solar system.

He claimed that the Sun was at the center and argued in favour of Earth and other bodies moving around it. His observations were published in the six books of the seminal work, *On the Revolutions of the Heavenly Orbs* in 1543. Another well-known astronomer named Galileo Galilei supported this model and strongly vouched for it. Observations made by him (and much later by others) through telescopes proved that the heliocentric theory was correct.

▶ A statue of Nicolaus Copernicus in Torun, Poland. Ironically, there is no record of Copernicus ever earning a bachelor's degree

The Majestic Milky Way

A large group or cluster of stars, gas, and dust held together by gravity is known as a galaxy. Galaxies are densely packed with billions of stars and their solar systems. On a dark, moonless night you will be able to see the majestic band of our Milky Way galaxy.

The solar system (of which Earth is a part) is only a small chunk of the Milky Way and lies far out within this galaxy. Just as Earth orbits the Sun, the Sun orbits the center of the Milky Way.

⭐ A Barred Spiral and its Contents

Based on their shapes, galaxies can be classified as spiral, elliptical, and irregular. Our Milky Way is a large, barred spiral and is flat. While most stars in the Milky Way exist alone or in pairs, there are several clearly visible groups of stars, each containing thousands of members. These are classified into **globular clusters**, **open clusters**, and **stellar associations**. The main difference between these groups is in the age and the number of their stars or members.

- Globular clusters are the largest amongst all the clusters and mainly consist of very old stars. The Milky Way has over 150 globular clusters or more.

- Smaller groups of stars that are not as big as globular clusters, and those which are mixed up along with the other majority of stars in the system, including the Sun, are known as open clusters. In comparison, they are young objects.

- Stellar associations are even younger than open clusters and are more loosely grouped together. They are usually not bound together by gravity and so do not form stable groups.

- The Milky Way also contains weak clouds of dust and gas called nebulas, which are the birthplace of most stars. It also contains indistinct objects which are the leftovers of the gas spewed out by exploding stars.

▲ Our home galaxy, the Milky Way

Isn't It Amazing!

The Sun and the solar system take 250 million years to complete one full rotation around the center of the Milky Way!

▲ The Milky Way galaxy rises over the MacDonald Observatory near Fort Davis, Texas, USA

The Scintillating Sun

The Sun is four-and-a-half billion years old. It is at a distance of 149,600,000 kilometres from Earth. It keeps the entire solar system together with the help of gravity. With a surface temperature of 10,000 degrees Fahrenheit, it is a source of light, heat, and energy for us on Earth, without which, no life could exist. So what is the Sun made up of and what does it do?

⭐ Structure and Layers of the Sun

The Sun has six layers. Gravitational force helps keep its huge mass together.

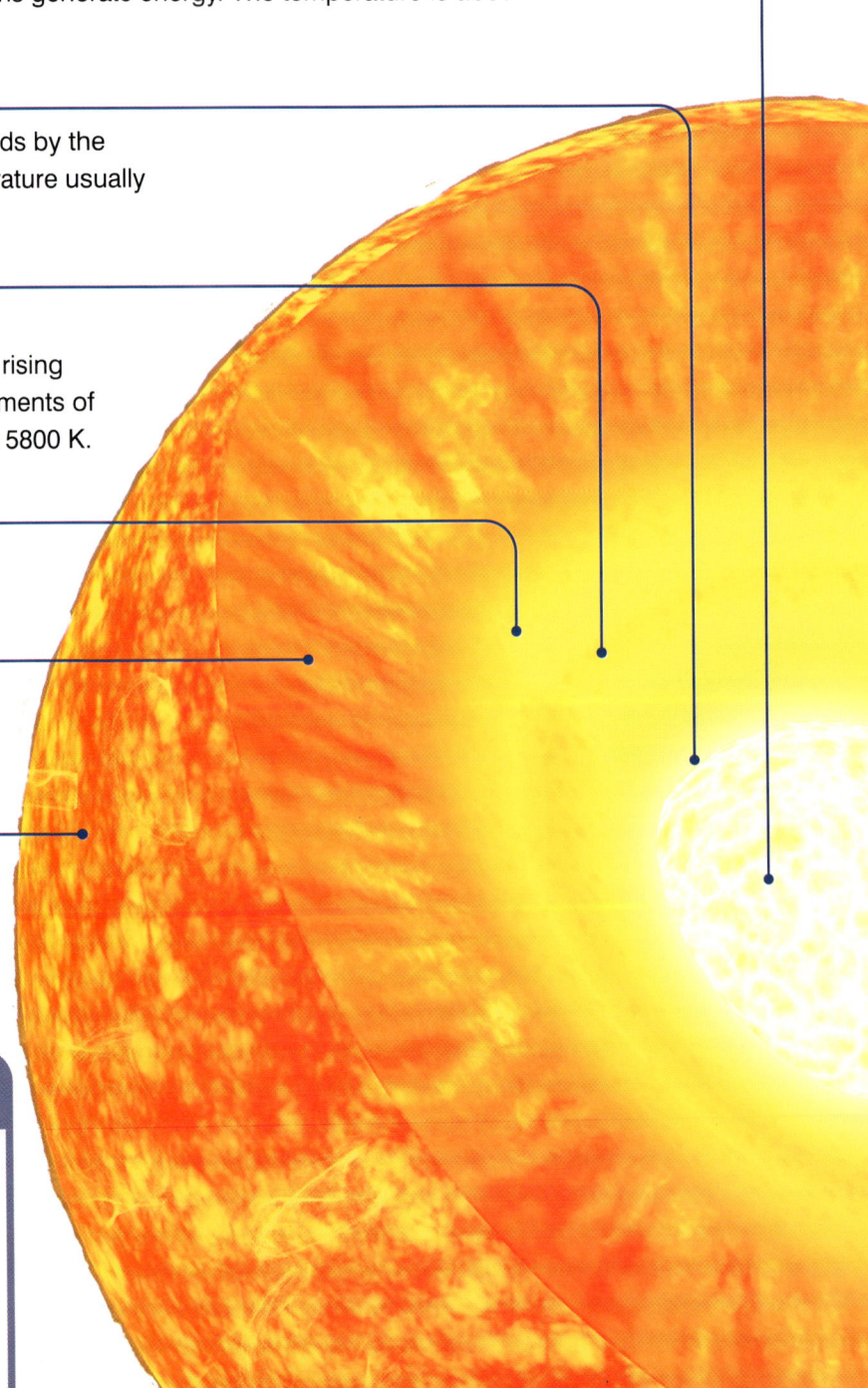

It is the innermost layer, where nuclear reactions generate energy. The temperature is about 15 million kelvin (K).

It is the zone where energy is released outwards by the process of radiation. Across this zone, temperature usually drops from about 7 million K to 2 million K.

Here energy is transported outwards by the mechanism of convection currents, which are rising movements of hot gas alongside falling movements of cool gas. Temperature falls from 2 million K to 5800 K.

It emits the light that we see with our eyes. Temperature is around 5800 K.

It lies above the photosphere and below the corona. From the inside to the outside edge, the temperature is around 4300 K to 8300 K.

It is the outermost layer and is extremely hot. On the outer disc of the Sun, there are filaments or **prominences,** which are dense, glowing, and intensely hot clouds. Temperature is around 2 million K.

👤 In Real Life

During solar activity, large quantities of energy (as high as 100 million K) and particles are released. Some of this reaches Earth, causing strong electrical currents that can damage satellites, rust pipelines, and harm power grids.

Size and Distance

The Sun is the largest and brightest object in the solar system. Compared to Earth, it is a giant! The radius of the Sun is 696,340 kilometres, whereas that of Earth is 6,378 km! It would take 1.3 million Earths to make up the entire volume of the Sun.

◄ The solar system was formed 4.6 billion years ago

 ## Solar Activity

The Sun is very active. This is particularly true at its surface, where it goes through a solar cycle or phases of being quiet or violently active. Very strong magnetic fields are generated by electrically charged gases that are found on its exterior. Since the gases on the Sun's surface are shifting all the time, they distort the magnetic fields. This distortion creates solar activity including solar wind, sunspots, and solar flares.

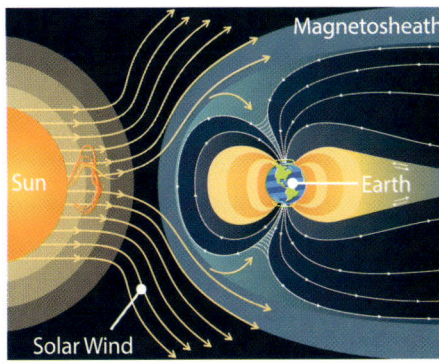

▶ A diagram showing solar wind activity and Earth's magnetic field

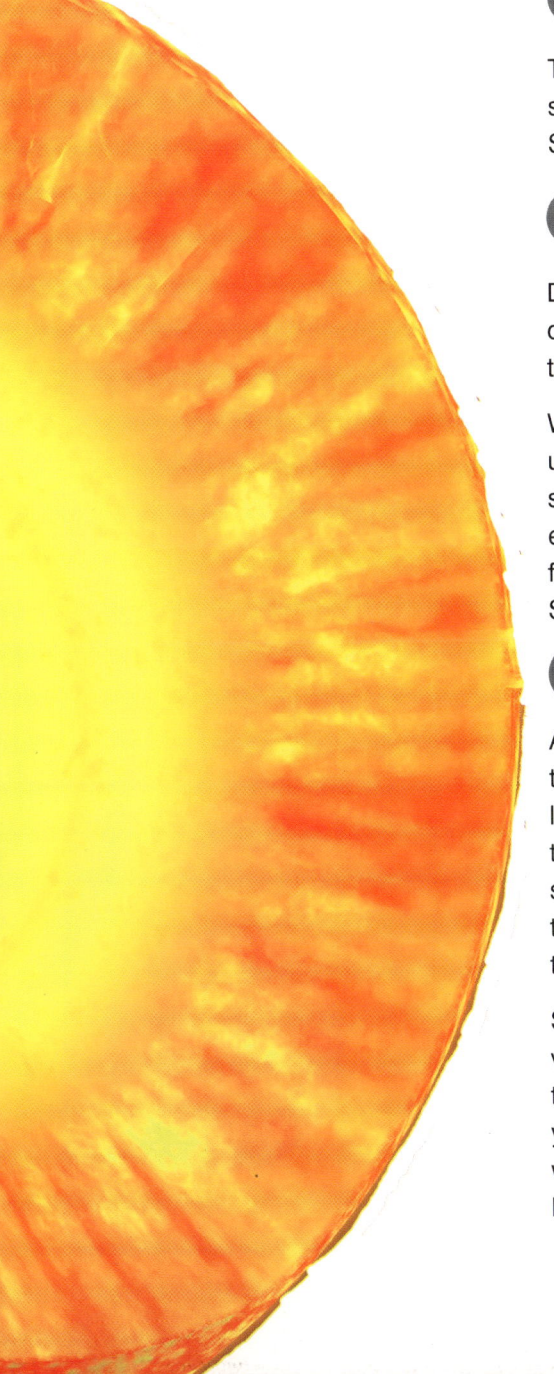

 ## Solar Wind

The Sun throws out a steady stream of particles and a magnetic field into space at high speeds known as solar wind. This creates a region around the Sun and the solar system called the **heliosphere**.

 ## Sunspots and Solar Flares

Dark spots on the surface of the Sun are known as sunspots. They appear dark because they are cooler as compared to the rest of the Sun, though their temperature is 3,800 K!

When the magnetic field lines are disturbed, sometimes it causes an unexpected explosion of energy known as a solar flare, which releases significant radiation into space. Sometimes, solar flares trigger a coronal mass ejection (CME) which are large bubbles of radiation and particles emanating from the Sun. They burst in space at great speeds due to the fluctuations in the Sun's magnetic field lines.

 ## Solar Eclipse

An eclipse takes place when a planet or a Moon comes in the way of the Sun's light. On Earth we experience two kinds—solar and lunar eclipses. When the Moon comes between Earth and the Sun and casts a shadow on our planet, it is called a solar eclipse. When this happens, it gets dark during the day. Depending on the degree to which it covers the Sun, it can be a partial or total eclipse.

Since the Moon's shadow cast on Earth is not very large, only some people on a small part of the planet will be able to see a solar eclipse. Also, you need to be on the side of Earth that has sunlight when this event takes place and be in the path of the Moon's shadow.

▲ The longest duration of a total solar eclipse is 7.5 minutes

Mercury
The Smallest and the Fastest Planet

The smallest planet in the solar system is Mercury. It is slightly bigger than Earth's Moon. It is the nearest planet to the Sun, but not the hottest.

Structure and Appearance

After Earth, Mercury is the second densest planet of our solar system. It has a huge metallic centre. Part of its core is liquid. Its outer shell is similar to that of Earth, comprising the mantle and crust. Mercury's surface looks like that of Earth's Moon. It has several **craters** (large bowl-shaped depressions) caused due to the impact of meteorites or comets striking its surface. It has stretches of smooth land and cliffs, and appears greyish-brown with bright streaks. Some regions near Mercury's poles never receive sunlight. These permanently shadowed regions are known to have water in the form of ice inside deep basin-like depressions.

▲ The inner structure of planet Mercury

In Real Life

Some craters and other features of Mercury are named after well-known authors like Dr Seuss, renowned musicians like Sergey Rachmaninoff and other artistes.

▼ Mercury is a rocky planet and has no moons

Unique Feature

Did you know that it takes only 88 Earth days for Mercury to finish one revolution around the Sun? Since it is so close to the Sun, a year on Mercury goes by pretty fast. Mercury's orbit around the Sun is three times closer than Earth's orbit around the Sun.

Like Earth, Mercury spins on its own axis. But it has a slow spin and only completes three rotations on its axis every two Mercury years. One complete rotation takes 59.65 Earth days or two-thirds of a Mercury year. As a result, a day lasts for almost two Mercury years! So, if you were standing on Mercury's surface, the Sun would pass overhead once during two revolutions around the Sun or once every 176 Earth days (*see Earth's movements on pp16–17*).

Quick Facts

- **Distance from the Sun:** 0.4 **astronomical units** (AU). One AU is the average distance between the Sun and Earth i.e., 150 million kilometres
- Time taken by light to travel from the Sun to Mercury: 3.2 minutes
- Surface temperatures: 430° C (day) -180° C (night)
- Atmosphere: None

Incredible Individuals

British astronomer and mathematician, Edmond Halley (1656–1742) was the first to compute the orbit of a comet, which was later called Halley's Comet, after him. He also noted the movement of Mercury across the Sun's sphere. His **star catalogue** (1678) was the first to identify the precise locations of southern stars obtained using a telescope.

Venus
The Hottest Planet

The second-closest planet to the Sun and the brightest in the solar system is Venus. It is one of the brightest objects (other than Earth's Moon), and so it can sometimes be seen in the night sky. It is slightly bigger than Earth and is also the closest planet to it. Venus is also called the 'Morning Star' or 'Evening Star' because it appears really bright from Earth during sunrise and sunset. However, it does not appear to twinkle. Instead, it glows with a steady light.

▲ *Venus is the second brightest natural object in the night sky after the Moon*

⭐ Structure and Appearance

The structure of Venus is similar to Earth, with an iron core and a mantle of hot rock with a thin crust-like surface which heaves and moves, creating volcanoes. This is because Venus is the hottest planet even though it is not the nearest to the Sun. Its thick atmosphere does not allow heat to escape; thus, Venus is burning hot. Even metals like lead would melt and become liquid there. It is an active planet with numerous volcanoes, large valleys, and mountains. Maxwell Montes is the highest mountain on Venus, rising to about 11 kilometres above the planet's mean radius. Two of its highland areas are around the same size as Australia and South America!

Due to its thick cloud covering, which reflects and disperses light from the Sun, Venus appears to be bright white in colour when it is viewed from space. But if you were standing on the surface of Venus, then it would look orangish since the same atmosphere filters the sunlight.

ⓘ Quick Facts

- **Distance from the Sun:** 0.7 AU
- Time taken by light to travel from the Sun to Venus: 6 minutes
- Surface temperatures: 471° C (hence there is no potential for life)
- Atmosphere: Thick layer of carbon dioxide and clouds of sulphuric acid.

— Crust
— Core
— Mantle

▲ *The internal structure of Venus*

⭐ Unique Features

Venus rotates in a direction opposite to Earth's and the other planets, except Uranus, i.e., from east to west. Like Mercury, it is very slow in its rotation and takes approximately 243 Earth days to spin on its axis once. But because it is near to the Sun, it takes only 225 Earth days to revolve around it.

Since the length of a day and a year is almost the same, the Sun rises twice during a year even though the day has not changed. Since Venus rotates backwards, the Sun rises in the west and sets in the east!

◄ *Maxwell Montes, the highest mountain of planet Venus*

Earth
The Habitable Planet

Earth, the third planet from the Sun, is the only known planet which is habitable by living beings. Liquid water is a crucial element that supports life, and so far, only Earth, the fifth-largest planet, has water on its surface. Amongst the four inner planets—Mercury, Venus, Earth, and Mars—composed mainly of metal and rock, Earth is the biggest.

⭐ Structure and Appearance

Earth has four major layers—the central core, the outer core, the mantle, and the crust. The solid core, where temperatures are really high, comprises iron and nickel. The outer core surrounding the inner one comprises molten iron and nickel. The mantle is sandwiched between the outer core and a fairly deep layer of crust.

Earth's surface is covered with mountains, valleys, volcanoes, and flat plains. The crust and the upper mantle of Earth form the lithosphere. It is broken up into giant plates. Earthquakes are caused by the shifting of these plates. Seventy per cent of Earth's surface is made up of oceans that contain 97 per cent of the planet's water.

▶ *Sometimes mountains such as the Himalayas are formed due to the plates ramming into each other*

⭐ Unique Features: Potential for Life

Earth has several ideal conditions or features that help support life on the planet. Besides liquid water, Earth's atmosphere is also important as it acts like a protective blanket around the planet. The atmosphere comprises 78 per cent nitrogen, 21 per cent oxygen, and 1 per cent other gases. This is a perfect balance of crucial gases to enable us to live and breathe. The average surface temperature on Earth is roughly 14°C, which is perfect for sustaining life. If there was no atmosphere, the temperature would have been much lower and unsuitable for living things. Water is able to exist in its liquid form for long periods due to the ideal temperature that is maintained by the atmosphere. Besides nourishing life on Earth, our atmosphere also protects us from the harmful radiation of the Sun. Although it is not very thick, it is sufficient to help burn up most of the meteoroids before they impact us on Earth. Another advantage of our atmosphere is that it is conducive for Earth's climate and weather.

▲ *The planet is home to several diverse species of living beings*

SPACE | SOLAR SYSTEM

◀ Earth as seen from space

ⓘ Quick Facts

- **Distance from the Sun:** Precisely 1 AU or 150 million kilometres
- **Time taken by light from the Sun to reach Earth:** 8 minutes
- **Average surface temperature:** 14°C
- **Number of Moons:** Unlike some planets that may have multiple Moons, Earth only has one

✦ Earth's Magnetosphere

The region around a planet that is ruled by the planet's magnetic field is known as a magnetosphere. The magnetosphere of Earth is an extensive, comet-shaped bubble and is an important factor that makes our planet habitable. While the other planets also have magnetospheres, amongst the rocky planets, Earth's magnetosphere is the strongest. The magnetosphere initially helped in developing life on Earth and continues to support and sustain it. It also acts as a protective shield against solar and cosmic radiation and prevents destruction of the atmosphere due to solar winds.

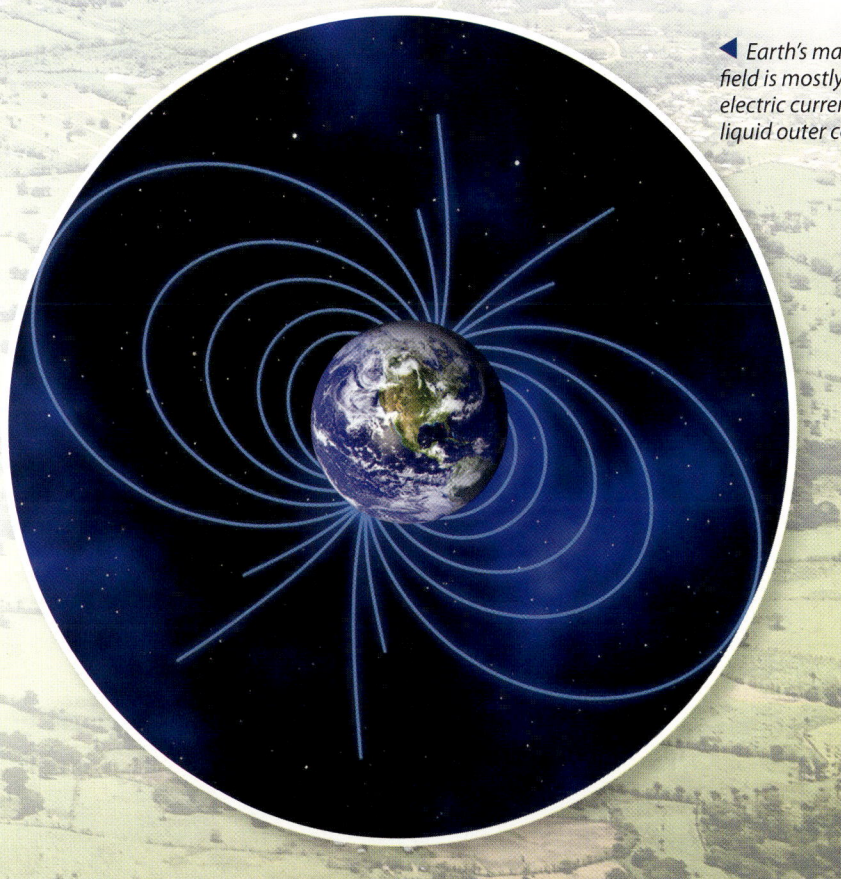

◀ Earth's magnetic field is mostly caused by electric currents in the liquid outer core

👤 In Real Life

The first creature or 'earthling' to orbit Earth in 1957 was the dog Laika. She did not survive the journey. Some years later, Belka and Strelka, two Soviet dogs, were the first living creatures to successfully return alive from space. This paved the way for human beings to explore the cosmos.

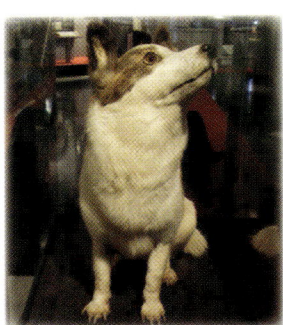

▲ *Strelka at Moscow's Memorial Museum of Cosmonautics*

Earth's Imaginary Lines

Did you know that Earth has imaginary lines running east-west and north-south to help pinpoint a location on it and tell time? Some imaginary lines are more important than others.

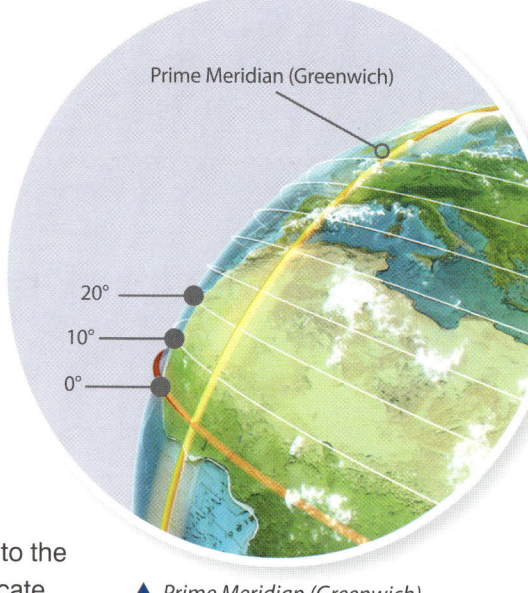
▲ *Prime Meridian (Greenwich)*

 ## Latitude and Longitude

The horizontal lines which run east-west are called latitudes and those that run north-south are longitudes. Together, using the latitude and longitude, we have formulated a grid system which helps us find the position or location of any place on Earth's surface. The most important latitude is the equator (0° latitude). It is a circle around Earth, equidistant from the north and south poles. It divides Earth into the northern and southern hemispheres. The other latitudes are a measurement to locate a place north or south of the equator.

Longitudes, also known as meridians, help measure the location of a place lying east or west of the **prime meridian**. The prime meridian is the most important longitude because it is the 0° longitude. It passes through the Observatory of Greenwich and divides Earth into the eastern and western hemispheres. In 1884, it was agreed upon as the prime meridian during an international conference in Washington, USA.

▲ *The Earth's axis*   ▲ *Longitude lines*   ▲ *Latitude lines*   ▲ *Earth's Equator*

 ## Universal System for Measuring Time and Date

Two longitudes which help establish a standard system for keeping time and date across the world are:

- The prime meridian or 0° longitude, which is the specially designated imaginary north-south line that passes through both the geographic poles.

- The International Date Line (IDL) or 180° longitude, which is another imaginary line running from the North Pole to the South Pole, but located on the opposite side of Earth from the prime meridian.

▼ *Royal Greenwich Observatory, London is the home of time and space*

International Date Line (IDL)

The IDL is a standard embraced globally. It was established in 1884 and passes through the mid-Pacific Ocean, zigging and zagging to keep nearby nations on their own day and date. When one crosses the IDL, the day and date change.

 # Establishing Time Zones

It was important to have a global standard of time and the need was felt particularly in the 19th century with the advent of the railways and other new industries. Sir Sandford Fleming (1827–1915) first created a system of using 24 standard time zones in 1876 and though not recognised by any global official body, by 1900 it led to the refined version and adoption of the time zone system used around the world today. Within each time zone, the clocks would be set at an average time that most closely reflected where the Sun was located in the sky.

The prime meridian serves as the basis for the world's standard time zone system. International time is measured in time zones which are 15 degrees apart (360 degrees divided by 24 hours equals 15 degrees per hour). They are numbered by the hour, starting from the prime meridian. So, the clock in Greenwich shows what is known as Greenwich Mean Time, now called the Universal Time Coordinated (UTC). This system makes it easy to calculate the time in other zones.

For example, Germany, which is one time zone east of Greenwich, will be labelled as 'GMT+1'. So, if the time in Greenwich is 10:00 a.m., the time in Germany will be 11:00 a.m. (10:00+1 hour).

California, which lies eight time zones to the west of Greenwich, will be labelled as 'GMT - 8'. So, the time in California will be 2:00 a.m. (10:00-8 hours).

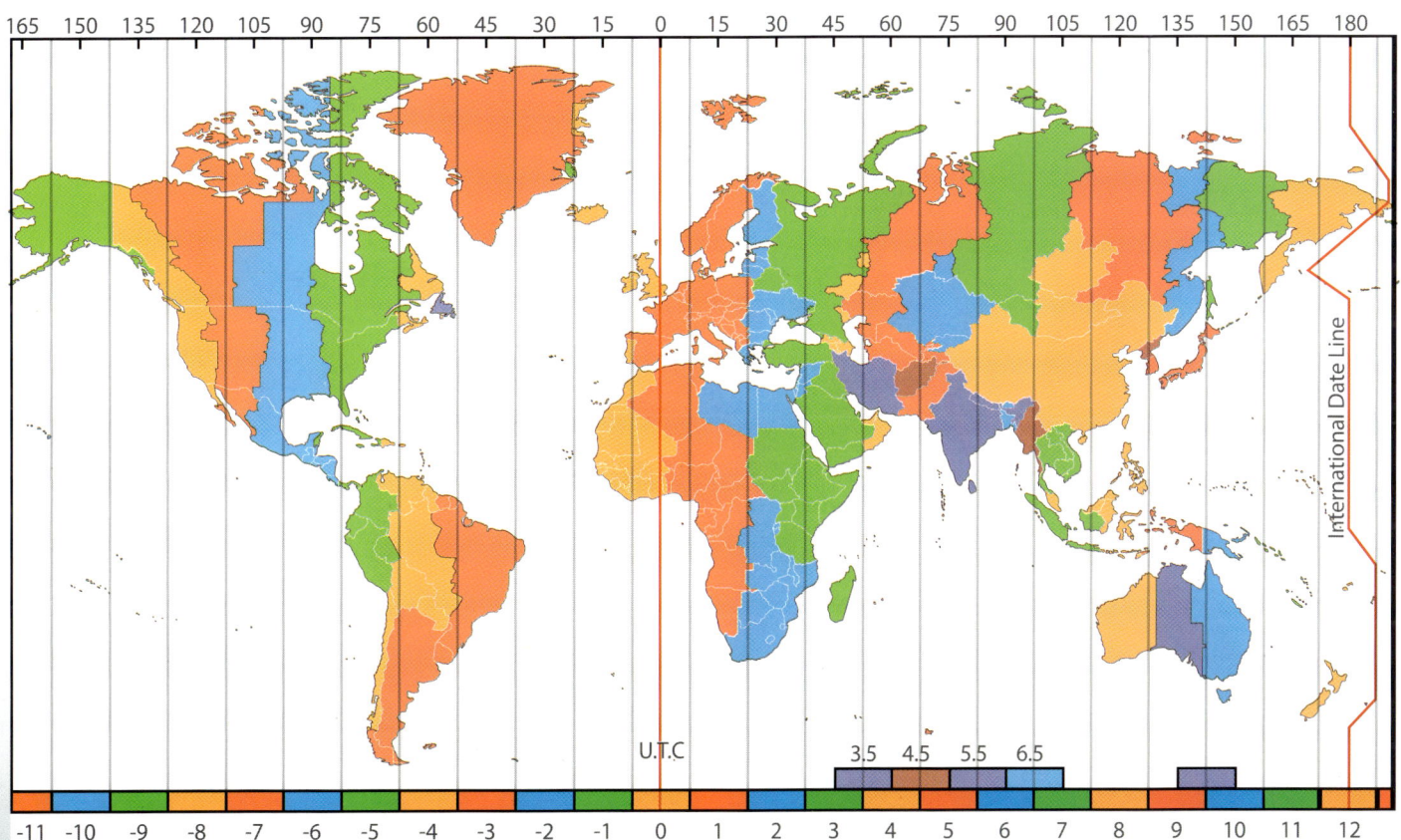

▲ *World time zones mapped on a flat surface. The time zone of each part can be determined by the colour-coded key placed at the bottom*

Earth's Movements

Earth's movement on its axis and around the Sun causes day and night and the seasons we experience. How does this happen?

Earth's Rotation

All planets rotate or spin on their own axis. Earth's rotation on its axis is what results in the phenomenon of day and night. When Earth rotates, one half of the planet faces the Sun at a particular time. The part that faces the Sun has light and experiences day, while the other half, which is in darkness, experiences night.

If observed from a point above the North Pole, you will see that Earth rotates in a counterclockwise fashion, from west to east. This is known as **prograde rotation**. Due to this direction of Earth's spinning, we see the Sun rising in the east every morning and setting in the west every evening. **Retrograde rotation**, on the other hand, is when a planet rotates in a clockwise direction.

Earth takes 23 hours and 56 minutes to complete one rotation, which makes up 24 hours, or one day and one night. However, since Earth's axis is slightly tilted at an angle of 23.44° and is not at a right angle with the Sun, not all places on Earth receive 12 hours of light and 12 hours of darkness every day.

Due to this tilting of Earth, there is a variation in the amount of daylight some parts of the planet receive. At the equator there is hardly any variation, but it is greatest in the region of the poles. Due to this, the poles never experience complete darkness during summers nor complete light during winters.

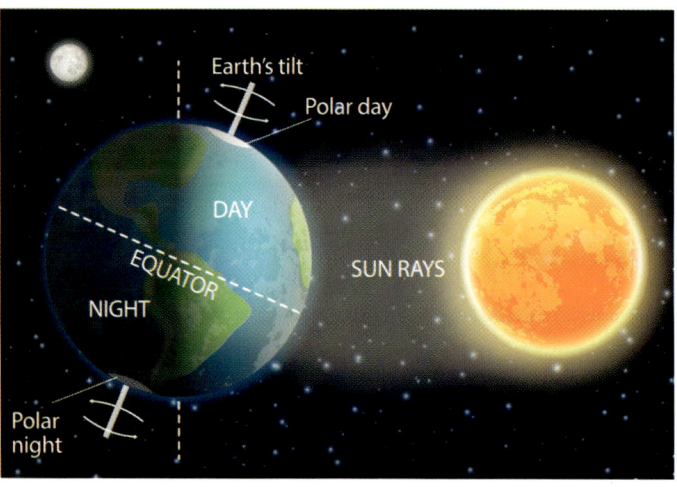
▲ The illustration shows the 24-hour day-and-night cycle of Earth

In Real Life

The word Earth is derived from Old English, Dutch, and Germanic words: eorthe, aarde, and erde respectively. Interestingly, unlike the other planets in the solar system, Earth's name does not originate from Greco-Roman mythology. The symbol often used to denote Earth is ♁.

▲ The various seasons of Earth: spring, summer, autumn, and winter

Earth's Revolution

Earth revolves around the Sun in an elliptical or oval-shaped orbit. It takes nearly 365.25 days to complete one full revolution. Since our calendar year comprises only 365 days, every four years an extra day called the leap day is added to the month of February to make up for the difference. That is why during a leap year, February has 29 days instead of 28.

The four seasons of spring, summer, autumn or fall, and winter are experienced on Earth due to two factors: the tilt of the planet and its rotation. The changing seasons do not depend on Earth's distance from the Sun.

Since Earth's axis is tilted and always points in the same direction, we have seasons. Starting from December for a period of approximately three months, people living in the northern hemisphere will experience winter, since during this time the Sun shines here indirectly. Meanwhile, those living in the southern hemisphere will experience summer, since it receives direct heat and light from the Sun during this time.

The opposite happens in the months beginning from June onwards, which is when the southern hemisphere will experience winter and the northern hemisphere will have summer for the same reasons.

However, you will experience the four seasons only if you are living in the middle latitudes (places which are not near the poles or the equator). If you live closer to the equator, you will experience hardly any change in the seasons and the duration of daylight and darkness will almost be the same the whole year. Such places mostly remain warm throughout the year and typically have alternating rainy and dry seasons.

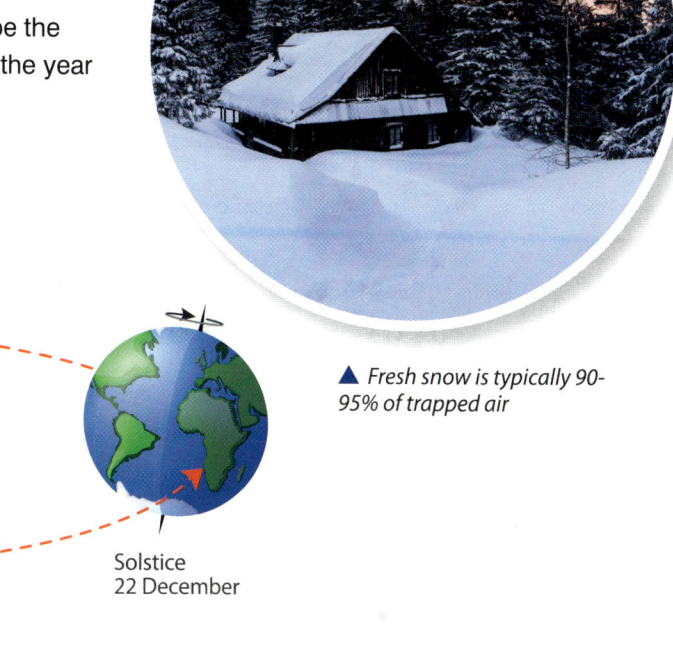

▲ Fresh snow is typically 90-95% of trapped air

▶ Earth's seasons in the northern hemisphere

Equinox 21 March
Earth's orbit
Solstice 21 June
Equinox 23 September
Solstice 22 December

Isn't It Amazing!

If you look very closely at a snowflake, you will find that it has a very pretty and delicate pattern. Snowflakes are usually hexagonal in shape and are formed by crystals of ice. Their sizes and shapes depend on the temperature and quantity of water vapour available as they grow.

▼ Sunflowers are famous for their heliotropism- the tendency to track the Sun

Earth's Moon

Earth's Moon is the brightest and largest object seen in the night sky from our planet. It plays an important role in making Earth habitable for all life on the planet.

 ## Formation, Structure, and Appearance

The Moon was formed when a body the size of Mars banged into Earth about 4.5 billion years ago. The debris that was generated collected together to form the Moon. Just like Earth, its Moon has a core, mantle, and crust. It has several inactive volcanoes.

Since the Moon has a very scanty atmosphere, asteroids, meteoroids, and comets constantly strike at its surface and create craters and due to a weak gravity, astronauts on the Moon tend to bounce around.

◀ *Structure of the Moon: crust, mantle, and core. The size of its core is only about 20% the size of the Moon*

▲ *Neil Armstrong after landing on the moon: 'One small step for man, one giant leap for mankind.'*

 ## The Importance of the Moon

The Moon is important because:
- It is the only place in space beyond Earth where human beings have landed
- It helps decrease Earth's wobble on its axis and helps create an equitable climate
- It is responsible for causing the tides.

 ## Lunar Eclipse

A lunar eclipse takes place when Earth comes in the way and prevents the Sun's light from reaching the Moon. So on such nights the full Moon is not visible because Earth's shadow covers it.

▼ *Lunar eclipses only occur during a full moon*

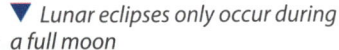

At times, the Moon may appear red during an eclipse. This is because Earth's atmosphere absorbs the other colours from the Sun's light while it bends the light in the direction of the Moon.

Although the Moon orbits Earth every month, a lunar eclipse does not take place every month. This is because the path of the Moon around Earth is tilted in comparison to Earth's orbit around the Sun and it does not always get inside Earth's shadow. So, even when the Moon's position is behind Earth, it can still receive light from the Sun.

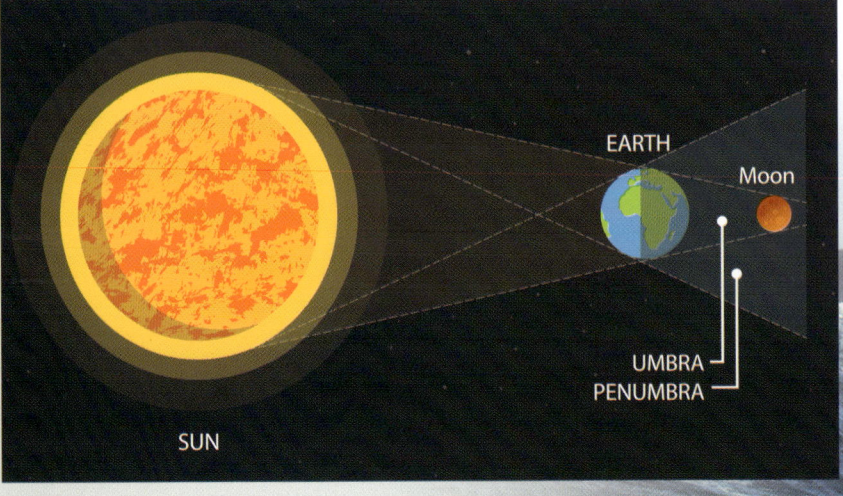

Viewing the Lunar Eclipse

Viewing a lunar eclipse is exciting and also special since it does not happen every month. It is a popular space activity that people go to watch. If you are located on the side of Earth that is experiencing night when the eclipse takes place, you will be able to view it.

To remember the difference between a solar eclipse and lunar eclipse, you should recall their names. Solar means Sun; during the solar eclipse, a shadow is cast on the Sun. Lunar means Moon; during a lunar eclipse, a shadow is cast on the Moon.

▲ *Lunar eclipses are more widely visible than solar eclipses*

Oceanic Tides

Tides are the rise and fall in the level of water in the oceans. They are caused because of Earth's rotation and the gravitational pull of the Sun and the Moon. Since the Moon is much closer to Earth, its gravitational pull is much stronger than the Sun's.

Tides are cyclical in nature—as the Moon rotates around Earth and the position of the Sun changes, the water levels in the sea constantly rise or fall. This cycle takes place either once (diurnal) or twice (semidiurnal) in a day.

High tide (when water comes gushing on to the shore) is caused by the gravity of the Moon on the part of Earth directly below the Moon, as well as on the opposite side of Earth. Low tide (when water recedes from the shoreline) takes place on the parts of Earth that are 90 degrees away from the Moon.

▲ *The outermost crust of the Moon has endured several asteroid impacts that have led to craters on its surface*

▼ *Some waves, called Tsunamis, are caused due to underwater earthquakes as well*

Phases of the Moon

Did you notice that the Moon appears to be a different shape every other night? Does it seemingly disappear from the night sky? In reality, the Moon does not change shape at all.

▲ A beautiful moonlit night

'Changing' Moon

The Moon does not emit light by itself. 'Moonlight' is actually the Sun's light reflected off the Moon's surface. Since it orbits Earth, different parts of the Moon get illumined by the Sun each night, which is why we see the different shapes.

The Moon completes one orbit around Earth in 27.3 days, but since Earth is also travelling around the Sun at the same time, it takes the Moon 29.5 days to go through the entire 8 phases that make up a lunar month. As it orbits Earth, we see varying combinations of the lit and dark parts of its surface. Specific configurations of dark and light are known as the Moon's phases.

▶ Phases of the Moon

First Quarter
In this phase, one half of the Moon is lit and it looks like the letter 'D'.

Waxing crescent
Waxing means the visible illuminated area increases from one day to the next and when part of the Moon's edge is lit but the rest of the surface appears dark.

Waxing Gibbous
In the waxing gibbous phase, the lit part of the Moon "is greater than a semi-circle but less than a circle."

Full Moon
The full Moon occurs when the Moon is on the opposite side of Earth from the Sun and we can see the complete illuminated round disc of the Moon.

New Moon
The new Moon occurs when the Sun and Moon are on the same side of Earth and we see only the dark side.

Waning Gibbous
Waning means the visible illuminated area decreases daily and the illuminated part of the Moon looks similar to waxing gibbous, but on the opposite side.

Last Quarter
In the last quarter, half of the Moon is illumined, looking like an opposite 'D'.

Waning Crescent
In the waning crescent phase, the illumined part of the Moon looks like the letter 'C' but most of the visible surface is dark.

Exploring Mars: The Red Planet

Mars is half the size of Earth. It is a cold desert world. It has clouds, winds, seasons, polar ice caps, volcanoes, canyons, and approximately a 24-hour day. This variety in features makes Mars one of the most explored bodies in the solar system.

Structure and Appearance

Its dense core is made up of iron, nickel, and sulphur. Its outer crust comprises iron, magnesium, aluminium, calcium, and potassium. A rocky mantle lies between the core and the crust. Mars appears to be red due to the rusting of iron found in the rocks, soil, and dust. The red dust flies into the atmosphere and makes the planet appear red.

Isn't It Amazing!

For the first time ever, sounds of the winds on the surface of Mars were captured and shared by NASA's InSight (Interior Exploration using Seismic Investigations, Geodesy and Heat Transport) lander in December 2018.

▲ NASA's InSight lander is the first outer space robotic explorer for Mars

▶ The red planet Mars is named after the Roman God of War

The Mystery of Mars

Billions of years ago, Mars may have had water and maybe even rivers and oceans. While there is still some water found on Mars, the atmosphere is too thin for it to last for a long time on its surface.

Since water is a prime indicator and essential pillar of life, this question of whether Mars supported microscopic life forms in the past remains a topic of debate.

Quick Facts

- **Distance from Sun:** 1.5 AU
- **Time taken by light from the Sun to reach Mars:** 13 minutes
- **Temperature:** 20° C to 153° C
- **Atmosphere:** Thin layer of carbon dioxide, argon, nitrogen, some oxygen, and water vapour

Incredible Individuals

German astronomer Johannes Kepler (1571–1630) is best known for discovering the three main laws of planetary motion. When Kepler discovered them, he did not call them 'laws' but considered them to be 'celestial harmonies' reflecting God's creation and design of the universe. They were recognized as laws after Isaac Newton expanded on them based on general physical principles.

Jupiter
A Giant among Planets

Jupiter is by far the largest planet in the solar system! It is approximately 139,820 km wide at its equator and more than twice the size of all the other planets put together.

⭐ Structure

Like the Sun, Jupiter is composed mainly of hydrogen and helium. Due to an increase in pressure and temperature in the atmosphere, it compresses the hydrogen gas into liquid form. This has resulted in Jupiter having the largest ocean in the solar system made up of hydrogen (not water). Scientists believe that halfway through the planet's centre, the pressure is so high that the liquid core gets charged and becomes a conductor of electricity.

Jupiter rotates very fast (taking about 10 hours to spin around once), and this causes electrical currents in this region. This fast movement is also thought to generate the planet's strong magnetic field. It has not yet been confirmed whether Jupiter has a central core that is solid, or one that is a thick, extremely hot, and dense liquid.

◀ Inner structure of planet Jupiter

Liquid hydrogen | metallic hydrogen | core | cloud layers

⭐ Appearance

Jupiter is a planet with colourful cloud bands and spots. Jupiter's atmosphere comprises three layers of clouds. The top layer is perhaps made of ammonia ice; the middle layer of ammonium hydrosulphide crystals; and the last layer of water ice and vapour. It does not have a solid surface.

Its brightly coloured bands may be caused by gases that contain sulphur and phosphorus, which rise up from the warm interior of the planet. It spins so fast that it generates powerful jet streams which distinguish the band of clouds into dark and bright regions. The planet is also characterised by exceptionally high-speed winds, especially at its equator.

Jupiter is a gas giant, it does not have a solid surface, but mostly comprises spiralling gases and liquids. A spacecraft would not have anywhere to land on Jupiter and would most likely disintegrate if it tried to land due to the planet's extremely hot temperature. The cloud temperature is about -145°C.

▲ Jupiter's atmosphere from Voyager 1

SPACE | SOLAR SYSTEM

Unique Features

Jupiter's cold whirling clouds and stripes made up of ammonia and water floating around in the atmosphere are its distinctive features. It is also known for its 'Great Red Spot'. This is a huge storm that has been swirling around for hundreds of years on the planet's surface. Jupiter is quite similar to a star but it did not get big enough for it to start burning like most stars do.

It has the shortest day in the solar system, lasting only 10 hours; however, it takes 12 Earth years or 4,333 Earth days to revolve around the Sun due to its size and distance from the Sun!

It is believed that by exerting its gravitational force on asteroids in the asteroid belt, Jupiter protects Mercury, Venus, Earth, and Mars and prevents large asteroids from crashing into them.

▲ Jupiter's famous eye-shaped Great Red Spot

In Real Life

Jupiter's rings were discovered in 1979 by NASA's Voyager 1 spacecraft. Scientists were surprised by this discovery, since they comprised small, dark particles which are not so easy to see except when the Sun lights it up from the back.

ⓘ Quick Facts

- **Distance from the Sun:** 5.2 AU
- Time taken for light to travel from the Sun to Jupiter: 43 minutes
- Moons: 79 confirmed moons; the four largest being—Io, Europa, Ganymede, and Callisto, also known as Galilean satellites since they were first observed by astronomer Galileo Galilei in 1610 using one of the earliest telescopes. Ganymede is Jupiter's largest moon and also the largest moon in the solar system

▲ Io   ▲ Europa   ▲ Ganymede   ▲ Callisto

23

Saturn
The Ringed Giant

With a diameter of about 116,460 kilometres, Saturn is the second-largest planet in the solar system. It looks regal and grand because of the icy rings that surround it.

Structure and Appearance

Saturn, a gas giant, comprises hydrogen and helium and has a dense center of iron and nickel. The speed of wind in the upper atmosphere can reach 1,800 kilometres, which is much greater than the most powerful winds generated by hurricanes on Earth. This is unique to Saturn within the solar system. Saturn's atmospheric pressure is so great that it forces gases to turn into liquid. Saturn has clouds, jet streams, and storms surrounding it and often takes on shades of yellow, brown, and grey.

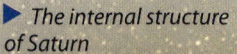
▶ The internal structure of Saturn

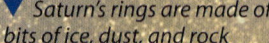
▼ Saturn's rings are made of bits of ice, dust, and rock

Isn't It Amazing!

The average density of Saturn is less than water. This means that if Saturn were put into a giant bathtub, it would float! Density is the amount of mass in a specified space. The denser an object, the less likely it is to float.

Quick Facts

- **Distance from Sun:** 9.5 AU
- Time taken by light from the Sun to reach Saturn: 80 minutes
- Moons: 53 confirmed moons and twenty nine more awaiting confirmation

Unique Features

Saturn has amazing rings comprising billions of pieces of ice and rock covered by dust. Some of these pieces are as large as mountains. The rings orbit the planet at different speeds and extend for nearly 282,000 kilometres from the planet! Most of the rings are fairly close together, except for a gap known as the Cassini Division between rings A and B. Rings A, B, and C are the main rings. Rings D, F, G, and E are fainter.

Saturn's atmosphere has a hexagon-shaped or six-sided jet stream which stretches for around 30,000 kilometres across, consisting of extremely high-speed winds and a swirling storm in the center. This feature is unique to Saturn and is not found anywhere else.

Incredible Individuals

Italian-born French astronomer, Gian Domenico Cassini (1625–1712) discovered four of Saturn's moons and found the dark gap between Saturn's rings A and B called the Cassini Division. He found the shadows of Jupiter's satellites, the flattening of its poles, and calculated the time taken by Mars for one rotation.

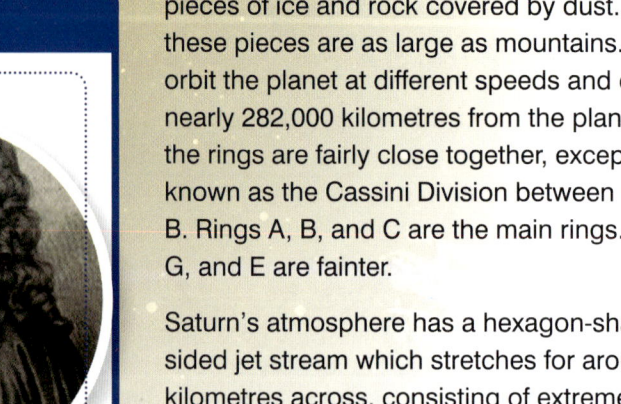

Uranus
The Planet that Spins Sideways

A cold and windy ice giant, Uranus is the seventh planet from the Sun and also the third largest from the Sun.

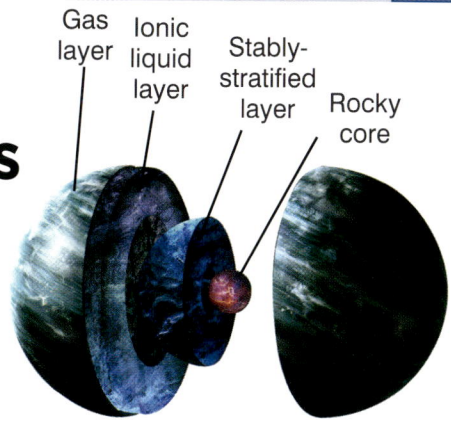

▲ *Internal structure of Uranus*

Structure and Appearance

It has an extremely hot (4,982° C), small rocky core. 80 per cent of its mass comprises a hot dense fluid of 'icy' materials including water, methane, and ammonia. Uranus does not have any land surface but is mainly a body of billowing fluids.

After Saturn, it is the second least dense planet. The atmosphere comprises hydrogen and helium, with small amounts of methane, water, and ammonia. Light from the Sun gets reflected back by the cloud cover of Uranus. The methane gas in the atmosphere absorbs the red part of the light and reflects a blue-green colour. Hence, Uranus appears to be bluish-green.

In a fly-by of Uranus in 1986, the spacecraft Voyager 2 noticed discrete clouds, the Great Dark Spot, and a few small dark spots. Recently, more vigorous clouds and some quick-changing bright features have been seen. Winds on Uranus can reach speeds of 900 kmph. The planet has 13 dim rings.

▼ *Astronomer William Herschel (1738–1822) discovered the planet Uranus*

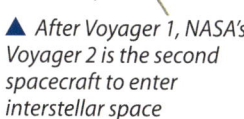

▲ *After Voyager 1, NASA's Voyager 2 is the second spacecraft to enter interstellar space*

Unique Features

Uranus rotates sideways on its axis at an almost 90° angle from the plane of its orbit. This unusual tilt makes it seem as if the planet is spinning on its side and causes the most extreme seasons found in the solar system.

Uranus was discovered in 1781 by astronomer William Herschel without a telescope. He thought it was a comet or a star. However, two years later it was recognised as a new planet by astronomer Johann Elert Bode, who gave it its name. Uranus and Venus are the only two planets that rotate from east to west.

▲ *Johann Elert Bode is also known for determining the orbit of Uranus*

ⓘ Quick Facts

- **Distance from the Sun:** 19.8 AU
- **Time taken by light from the Sun to reach Uranus:** 2 hours and 40 minutes
- **Planetary atmosphere:** A minimum temperature of -224.2° C
- **Moons:** 27 confirmed moons named after characters from the works of William Shakespeare and Alexander Pope

Neptune
The Windy Planet

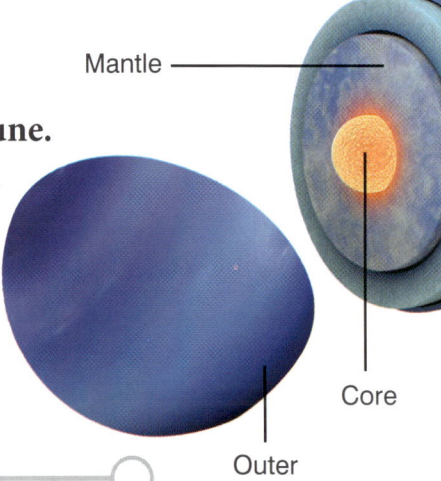
Mantle
Core
Outer atmosphere

▲ *Inner structure of Neptune*

The last major planet and farthest away from the Sun is Neptune. It is more than 30 times farther than Earth. It is the only planet which cannot be seen by the unaided eye and was actually discovered through careful mathematical calculations. Neptune has only completed one orbit around the Sun, in 2011, since its discovery way back in 1846. Each orbit takes 165 years to complete.

⭐ Structure and Appearance

Very similar in structure to Uranus, Neptune is mostly made up of dense fluids of 'icy' material comprising water, methane, and ammonia which surrounds a small rock-like core. Neptune is the densest planet amongst the giant ones.

Underneath Neptune's cold clouds, scientists think that there may exist an ocean of extremely hot water which does not boil and evaporate due to the intense high pressure that keeps it locked in. This planet too does not have a solid surface but has an atmosphere of hydrogen, helium, and methane, which is quite extensive. This slowly merges into water and other melted ice lying over a heavy, solid core, whose mass is the same as that of Earth.

Neptune is a cold, dark planet. It is so far from the Sun that during peak midday, the sky looks like it is almost time for the Sun to set. Since it is so far away, light from the Sun hardly reaches it. In fact, the sunlight we see on Earth is 900 times brighter! Unlike Uranus, which looks bluish-green in colour, Neptune appears to be bright blue.

▼ *Neptune is about four times wider than Earth*

Unique Features

Neptune has supersonic gusts of wind swirling around it. In fact, it is the windiest planet in the entire solar system. Even though it is so far away from the Sun and only receives very low energy inputs from it, the planet's wind speeds are three times stronger than those of Jupiter and nine times stronger than those seen on Earth. Neptune's winds travel at a speed of 2,000 kmph.

The Great Dark Spot, an oval-shaped storm, was discovered in 1989 in the planet's southern hemisphere and was so huge that it could hold the whole of Earth in it. That storm has since died but there are new ones which keep forming in different regions.

Triton, the largest moon of Neptune, is a very icy cold body and is the only large-sized moon that orbits its planet in a direction opposite to the planet's rotation. This indicates that earlier it may have been a separate object but was later seized by Neptune.

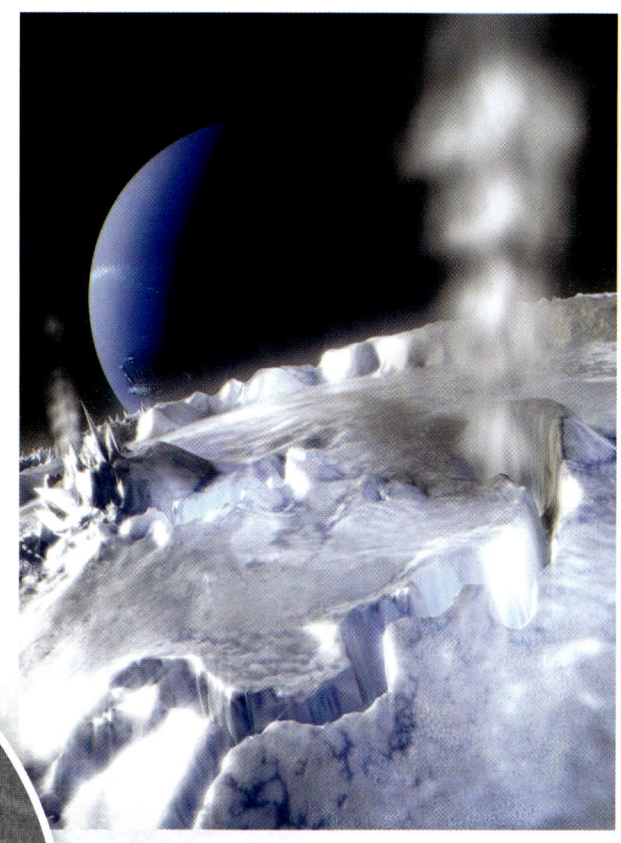

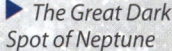
The Great Dark Spot of Neptune

Neptune seen from its moon Triton's icy surface

Quick Facts

- **Distance from the Sun:** 30 AU
- Time taken for light from the Sun to reach Neptune: 4 hours
- Moons: 14 moons, named after lesser sea gods and nymphs from Greek mythology

Isn't It Amazing!

Neptune experiences seasons similar to what we have on Earth since its axis of rotation is tilted at around 28° in relation to the plane of its orbit around the Sun. This is similar to our planet. The only difference is that one year—or the time taken by Neptune to revolve around the Sun—takes 165 Earth years or 60,190 Earth days. The four seasons, therefore, last for more than 40 years on Neptune!

The Kuiper Belt and the Oort Cloud

Beyond Neptune, the farthest planet from the Sun, there exists a ring of icy objects known as the Kuiper (pronounced Kai-pur) Belt. Beyond the Kuiper Belt lies the region known as the Oort Cloud. Comets originate from these regions.

⭐ The Kuiper Belt

The Kuiper Belt, a doughnut-shaped region, comprises pieces of rock, ice, comets, and dwarf planets including Pluto, Eris, Makemake, and Haumea. It is one of the largest structures in the solar system. The floating objects in the Kuiper Belt are known as Kuiper Belt objects (KBOs) or trans-Neptunian objects (TNO).

Isn't It Amazing!

In January 2019, NASA's New Horizons mission revealed the first detailed pictures of Kuiper Belt object Ultima Thule—the farthest object ever explored. This was a momentous accomplishment in the history of space exploration—no other spacecraft team has been able to trace such a tiny object moving at such great speed, located so far in outer space.

▲ NASA's New Horizons was the first mission to explore the Kuiper Belt. In 2015 it flew past dwarf planet Pluto, which is its most famous object

Incredible Individuals

Dutch-American astronomer Gerard Peter Kuiper (1905–1973) is well-known for several significant astronomical observations and discoveries. Between 1944 and 1949, he discovered the presence of methane gas in the atmosphere of Titan, Saturn's moon; correctly predicted the presence of carbon dioxide in Mars's atmosphere, and discovered that the rings of Saturn comprised ice particles.

In 1943, Kenneth Edgeworth (1880–1972), an Irish astronomer, had guessed that the solar system's smaller bodies extended beyond Pluto, but it was Kuiper who made a stronger case for their existence in 1951 and proposed the possible presence of this disc-shaped belt of comets orbiting the Sun. This was confirmed in the 1990s and the Kuiper Belt was named after him.

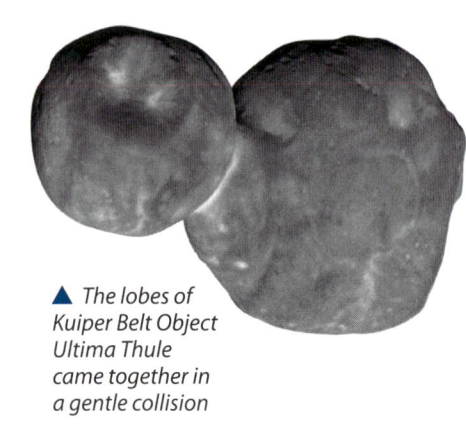

▲ The lobes of Kuiper Belt Object Ultima Thule came together in a gentle collision

⭐ The Oort Cloud

It is a huge spherical bubble surrounding the Sun, planets, and KBOs. It lies very far away; way beyond Pluto, on the outermost edges of the Kuiper Belt. It comprises ice-like bodies that can be larger than a mountain. It was named after Dutch astronomer Jan Oort who first suggested its existence in 1950.

Scientists think that the Oort Cloud may contain trillions of cold icy objects. Sometimes, some force disturbs these bodies and they begin to fall towards the Sun. ISON and Siding Spring are two examples of comets that originated from the Oort Cloud. ISON was destroyed on its way to the Sun, and Siding Spring may not return to the inner regions of the solar system for about 740,000 years.

Since this region is extremely far away, it has never been directly observed or discovered. Numerous comets originating from the Oort Cloud have been studied, but no space missions have been sent there.

🏅 Incredible Individuals

Jan Hendrik Oort (1900–1992) was a Dutch astronomer whose work in the 20th century helped us understand the Milky Way galaxy better. In 1927, Oort was able to confirm the theory that the Milky Way rotates in its plane around the center. He used radio astronomy to calculate the distance of the Sun from the center of the galaxy (30,000 light years). Radio astronomy is the study of celestial objects according to the radio-frequency energy emitted or reflected by them.

▶ The New York Times called Jan Hendrik Oort "one of the century's foremost explorers of the universe"

👤 In Real Life

The Oort Cloud is so far away that it would take the spacecraft Voyager 1 around 300 years to reach the inside of the Cloud, travelling at 1.6 million kilometres per day. It is so thick that it would probably take another 30,000 years to get to the farthest side of the Cloud.

▲ Comet Siding Spring was discovered on 3 January, 2013

▲ Comet ISON was discovered on 21 September 2012

The Dwarf Planets

Planets which did not quite make the cut of a 'regular' planet are dwarf planets. Pluto, Makemake, Haumea, Eris, and Ceres are dwarf planets. Ceres lies in the asteroid belt between Mars and Jupiter. All the others lie in the Kuiper Belt.

⭐ Pluto

Earlier classified as the ninth planet, Pluto was officially reclassified as a dwarf planet in 2006 by the International Astronomical Union (IAU).

Pluto has multifaceted features including tall mountains, long troughs and valleys, plains, large craters, and perhaps glaciers. It has a rocky core covered with a mantle of water ice. A thin layer of methane and nitrogen ice covers its surface.

It has a thin atmosphere of molecular nitrogen and traces of methane and carbon monoxide. Its atmosphere tends to expand when near the Sun but breaks down when far away. Closer to the Sun, the surface ice sublimates—it changes directly from a solid to a gaseous state. Unusually, Pluto orbits around the Sun on an elliptical path and is tilted.

⭐ Eris

Eris is one of the largest dwarf planets. Scientists are not sure of its structure, but it seems to have a rocky surface and its surface temperatures may range from -217°C to -243°C. Eris is so far away from the Sun that when it travels closer to it during an orbit, its icy atmosphere actually begins to thaw out. Due to the heat from the Sun, the atmosphere of Eris collapses. Then, when its distance from the Sun increases again, the atmosphere becomes frozen and falls to the surface as snow. Again, when it gets closer to the Sun, the atmosphere melts. One revolution around the Sun takes 557 Earth years. This dwarf planet has one moon.

⭐ Haumea

Haumea is approximately the same size as Pluto. It is one of the fastest rotating large objects in the solar system. This spin causes its shape to appear distorted like a football. Not much is known about its structure, surface, or atmosphere, but it may have a rocky surface with a layer of ice. One revolution around the Sun takes 285 Earth years. Since it spins so fast it finishes one rotation in four hours. It has two moons.

Eris image credits: ESO/L. Calçada and Nick Risinger (skysurvey.org)

Ceres

Ceres is the largest body in the asteroid belt between Mars and Jupiter. It makes up 25 per cent of the region's mass. It is the only dwarf planet which lies in the inner solar system and was the first object to be discovered there in 1801.

Ceres is more like the four terrestrial planets than its asteroid neighbours, only less dense. It has a layered interior, a solid core, and a water-ice mantle. Its crust is rocky, dusty, and has deposits of salts. The surface of Ceres is dotted with numerous small but young craters.

Ceres has a thin layer of atmosphere and there is proof to show that it contains water vapour, which makes it interesting to scientists who are keen to explore it.

Makemake

Isn't It Amazing!

Scientists think that the asteroid belt has a minimum of 40,000 asteroids that are 0.8 kilometres wide! Sometimes planets exert so much gravitational pull on an asteroid that it gets sucked from its belt and begins to orbit around the planet, just like a moon.

Makemake

Makemake is smaller than Pluto and the second brightest after Pluto, when seen from Earth. Not much is known about its structure. It cannot be studied in detail due to its distance, but it seems to have a reddish-brown colour. Frozen methane and ethane have been discovered on its surface. It may have a thin atmosphere of nitrogen. One revolution around the Sun takes 305 Earth years. One day on it is similar to a day on Earth.

Incredible Individuals

At the age of 25, Soviet cosmonaut Gherman Stepanovich Titov (1935–2000) became the youngest person to travel to space aboard the Vostok 2 mission in 1962. He piloted the first manned spaceflight of more than one orbit on the Vostok 2 spacecraft.

Word Check

Astronomical unit (AU): It is the average distance between the Sun and Earth, which is approximately 150 million km.

Chromosphere: It is the layer of the solar atmosphere that is located above the photosphere and beneath the transition region and the corona. The chromosphere is hotter than the photosphere but not as hot as the corona.

Convective zone: It is a layer in a star in which convection currents are the main mechanism by which energy is transported outwards. In the Sun, a convection zone extends from just below the photosphere to about 70 per cent of the solar radius.

Core: In solar astronomy, it is defined as the innermost part of the Sun, where energy is generated by nuclear reactions.

Corona: It is the outermost layer of the solar atmosphere. The corona consists of a highly rarefied gas with a temperature greater than one million kelvin. It is visible to the naked eye during a solar eclipse.

Coronal mass ejection (CME): They are huge bubbles of radiation and particles from the Sun. They explode into space at a very high speed when the Sun's magnetic field lines suddenly reorganise.

Crater: It is a circular depression in the surface of a planetary body. Most craters are the result of impacts of meteorites or of volcanic explosions on the surface.

Galaxy: It is a system of billions of stars (sometimes millions) grouped with dust and gas particles that are held together by gravitational attraction.

Globular clusters: They are old systems containing hundreds of thousands of stars closely packed in a symmetrical, roughly spherical form.

Heliosphere: It is the region surrounding the Sun and the solar system that is filled with solar magnetic field and the protons and electrons of solar wind.

Interplanetary medium: It is thinly scattered matter that exists between the planets and other bodies of the solar system, as well as the forces (e.g., magnetic and electric) that pervade this region of space.

Magnetic field: It is the area of influence of a magnet. It covers the whole area in which the attraction or repulsion of a magnet can be felt. Magnetic fields such as that of Earth cause magnetic compass needles and other permanent magnets to line up in the direction of the field.

Nebula: It is a large cloud of gas and dust that is formed in outer space.

Open cluster: It is a group of around 1,000 or more stars formed from the same giant molecular cloud. The stars are still loosely bound to each other by gravity.

Photosphere: It is the visible surface of the Sun. It consists of the zone in which the gaseous layers change from being totally opaque and blocking light, to a radiative condition, and then to being transparent and allowing light to pass through. It is the layer from which the light that we actually see is emitted.

Planetary system: It is a group of smaller bodies, like asteroids and planets that orbit around one or more stars. The solar system is a planetary system.

Prime Meridian: It is the 0 degree longitude near the middle of Earth, dividing it into the western hemisphere and eastern hemisphere.

Prograde rotation: It is the counter-clockwise movement of rotating and orbiting celestial bodies when viewed from a point above the North Pole.

Prominences: These are dense clouds of incandescent ionized gas projecting from the Sun's chromosphere into the corona.

Radiative zone: It is the interior layer of the Sun, lying between the core and the convection zone, where energy travels outward by radiation.

Retrograde rotation: All planets except Venus and Uranus rotate like the Sun, in the counter-clockwise direction. The two planets Venus and Uranus rotate in a clockwise direction, this is referred to as retrograde rotation.

Stellar association: It is a loose cluster of 10 or 100 stars that move together and share a common origin.